THE OFFICIAL
SOUTHAMPTON
FOOTBALL CLUB
ANNUAL 2019

SOUTHAMPTON FC

Written by Mark Perrow
Designed by Paul Galbraith and John Anderson

A Grange Publication

© 2018. Published by Grange Communications Ltd., Edinburgh, under licence from Southampton Football Club. Printed in the EU.

Photographs © Southampton FC / Getty Images / Reuters

ISBN: 978-1-912595-18-1

CONTENTS

SOUTHAMPTON FOOTBALL CLUB ANNUAL 2019!

WE'RE BRINGING YOU A HOST OF FUN FEATURES FOR SAINTS FANATICS TO ENJOY – WHATEVER YOUR AGE!

We start with a look back at a character-building 2017/18 season in which the club showcased its togetherness to overcome adversity, ensuring we can all enjoy another year of Premier League football at St Mary's.

We've broken the season down into our favourite moments and picked our top five goals, assists, saves and matches, as well as revealing who were the top-performing Saints on the pitch.

On top of that, we've got a whole new selection of quizzes and games for you to test your knowledge, as well as some inside tips on how to improve your own football performance.

We introduce you to our five summer signings – and the boss, who signed a new long-term contract before the start of the new season – while we asked a collection of Saints players to dish the dirt on their teammates!

If that wasn't enough, we've got all the best behind-the-scenes photos you've never seen, and everything you need to know about Saints' 2018/19 Premier League opponents.

Enjoy your read!

UNUSUALLY, SAINTS WOULD BEGIN THE 2017/18 CAMPAIGN WITH THREE CONSECUTIVE HOME GAMES.

A frustrating stalemate on the opening day against Swansea in which Saints did everything but score preceded the visit of West Ham to St Mary's.

The London Stadium's staging of the World Athletics Championships meant the Hammers would be forced to play away, leaving Saints with a six-week period without a home match later in the season.

What followed was a five-goal classic, as ten-man West Ham mounted an unlikely comeback from 2-0 down, only to be beaten by Charlie Austin's coolly-taken penalty deep into stoppage time.

The third home instalment signalled a premature end to Saints' hopes of repeating their EFL Cup Final heroics of the previous season, as Championship big spenders Wolves sprung a surprise.

A second goalless draw in Saints' first away examination at newly-promoted Huddersfield ensured Mauricio Pellegrino's men signed off the first month unbeaten in the league.

AUGUST

▶ FIXTURES ◀

SAINTS 0-0 **SWANSEA** Ⓓ

SAINTS 3-2 **WEST HAM** Ⓦ

SAINTS 0-2 **WOLVES** Ⓛ
CARABAO CUP R2

HUDDERSFIELD 0-0 **SAINTS** Ⓓ

▶▶ LEAGUE ◀◀

6	Chelsea	3	+2	6
7	Watford	3	+2	5
8	SAINTS	3	+1	5
9	Tottenham	3	+1	4
10	Burnley	3	0	4

MOMENT OF THE MONTH

Maya Yoshida and Charlie Austin celebrate after the striker's last-gasp spot-kick.

Southampton's unbeaten Premier League start was cut short by Watford, the early season surprise package under Marco Silva, who triumphed through two long-range goals at St Mary's.

Saints responded with their first away victory, preventing a new manager 'bounce' for Roy Hodgson, whose Crystal Palace side were still left waiting for their first point and first goal after skipper Steven Davis struck the winner inside six minutes at Selhurst Park.

The visit of Manchester United to St Mary's produced another encouraging display, but Romelu Lukaku's poacher's effort in the first half was enough for United to stay level on points with neighbours City at the top.

At Stoke, Saints would pit their wits against future boss Mark Hughes, who saw his side edge in front before Fraser Forster saved Saido Berahino's penalty.

Maya Yoshida's acrobatic volley then hauled the visitors level, only for Saints old boy Peter Crouch to arrive off the bench to deadly effect late on.

SEPTEMBER

> FIXTURES <

SAINTS 0-2 WATFORD Ⓛ

CRYSTAL PALACE 0-1 SAINTS Ⓦ

SAINTS 0-1 MAN UTD Ⓛ

STOKE 2-1 SAINTS Ⓛ

>> LEAGUE <<

10	West Brom	7	-2	9
11	Huddersfield	7	-2	9
12	SAINTS	7	-2	8
13	Stoke	7	-4	8
14	Brighton	7	-4	7

MOMENT OF THE MONTH

Maya Yoshida wheels away after his acrobatic volley levels the scores at Stoke.

Curtailed by the second international break of the season, October was shortened to just three matches, from which Saints won one and drew two.

Trailing to Newcastle at half-time, Manolo Gabbiadini created a goal out of

nothing to level the scores, only for Ayoze Pérez to fire the Magpies back in front straight from kick-off.

After Gabbiadini's second from the penalty spot earned a point at St Mary's, Saints were back on home turf and on course for another draw against West Brom until Sofiane Boufal took matters into his own hands.

Leaving a trail of defenders in his wake, the Moroccan ran half the length of the pitch before slotting home a stunning winner five minutes from time.

The month concluded with a first top-flight meeting with south coast neighbours Brighton in 35 years, as Steven Davis scored another early goal on the road in a 1-1 draw at the Amex Stadium.

OCTOBER

11

>· FIXTURES ·<

SAINTS 2-2 NEWCASTLE Ⓓ

SAINTS 1-0 WEST BROM Ⓦ

BRIGHTON 1-1 SAINTS Ⓓ

>>· LEAGUE ·<<

8	Watford	10	-3	15
9	Newcastle	10	+1	14
10	SAINTS	10	-1	13
11	Leicester	10	0	12
12	Brighton	10	-1	12

MOMENT OF THE MONTH

Sofiane Boufal celebrates his brilliant solo goal to defeat West Brom at St Mary's.

November began with Saints the latest victims of a smash-and-grab raid from high-flying Burnley, as Southampton-born Sam Vokes headed a late winner at St Mary's.

Anfield has been a happy hunting ground in recent times, but Liverpool were in no mood to be generous, starting their "fab four" of Philippe Coutinho, Sadio Mané, Mohamed Salah and Roberto Firmino.

The prolific Salah struck twice before the interval, while Coutinho added a third against a Saints side who bounced back in style against Everton, as Charlie Austin marked his first league start of the season with a brace.

Austin's two headers – carbon copies – were sandwiched between further goals from Dušan Tadić and Steven Davis as the Merseysiders were brushed aside at St Mary's.

Confidence restored, Saints were seconds away from an excellent point at runaway leaders Man City, only for Raheem Sterling to strike six minutes into added time to secure City's 19th successive victory.

NOVEMBER

>> FIXTURES <<

SAINTS 0-1 BURNLEY (L)

LIVERPOOL 3-0 SAINTS (L)

SAINTS 4-1 EVERTON (W)

MAN CITY 2-1 SAINTS (L)

>> LEAGUE <<

9	Leicester	14	-1	17
10	Brighton	14	-1	17
11	SAINTS	14	-3	16
12	Newcastle	14	-6	15
13	Everton	14	-11	15

MOMENT OF THE MONTH

Dušan Tadić shows what it means to make the breakthrough against Everton.

Charlie Austin continued where he'd left off against Everton with goals in 1-1 draws against Bournemouth and Arsenal, who were fortunate not to be further behind before Olivier Giroud pounced two minutes from time.

Less than three weeks after putting four past Everton, Saints found themselves on the receiving end as Claude Puel's Leicester proved too quick on the counter-attack, scoring three times in the first half en route to a 4-1 win.

Saints made life difficult for reigning champions Chelsea, but Marcos Alonso's curling free-kick in first-half stoppage time condemned them to back-to-back defeats.

Frustration ruled again when Huddersfield came from behind to earn a point at St Mary's, with goalscorer Austin hobbling off injured.

Harry Kane then fired his second successive hat-trick as Spurs hit five at Wembley, but Saints shored things up when Alex McCarthy marked his league debut for the club with a clean sheet at Old Trafford.

DECEMBER

>> FIXTURES <<

BOURNEMOUTH 1-1 SAINTS (D)

SAINTS 1-1 ARSENAL (D)

SAINTS 1-4 LEICESTER (L)

CHELSEA 1-0 SAINTS (L)

SAINTS 1-1 HUDDERSFIELD (D)

TOTTENHAM 5-2 SAINTS (L)

MAN UTD 0-0 SAINTS (D)

>> LEAGUE <<

11	Huddersfield	21	-14	24
12	Brighton	21	-10	22
13	SAINTS	21	-10	20
14	Bournemouth	21	-12	20
15	Stoke	21	-23	20

MOMENT OF THE MONTH

Charlie Austin's fine form continues as he fires home the equaliser at Bournemouth.

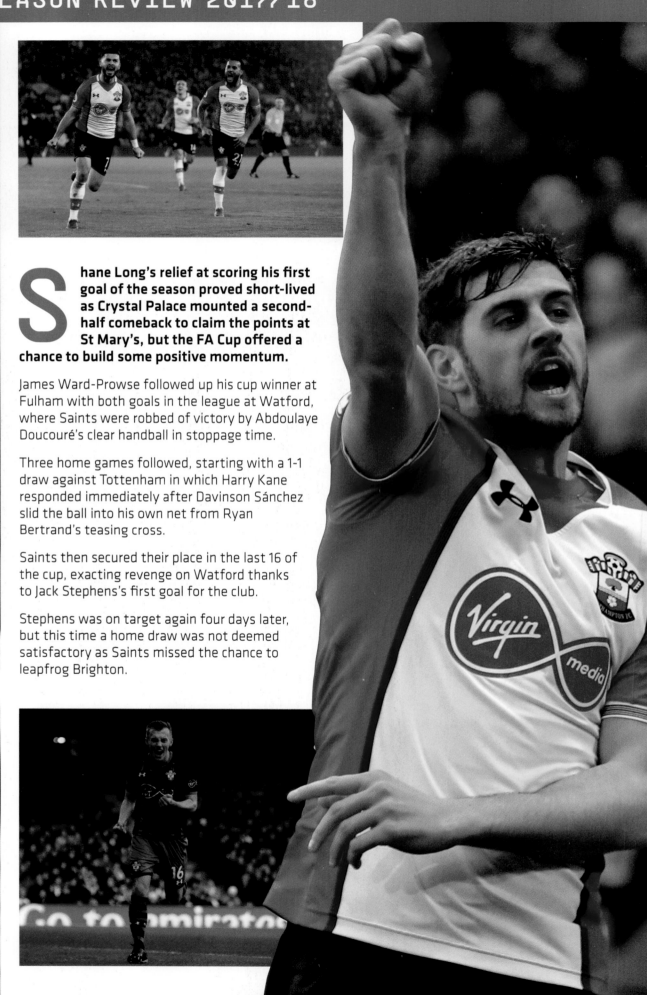

Shane Long's relief at scoring his first goal of the season proved short-lived as Crystal Palace mounted a second-half comeback to claim the points at St Mary's, but the FA Cup offered a chance to build some positive momentum.

James Ward-Prowse followed up his cup winner at Fulham with both goals in the league at Watford, where Saints were robbed of victory by Abdoulaye Doucouré's clear handball in stoppage time.

Three home games followed, starting with a 1-1 draw against Tottenham in which Harry Kane responded immediately after Davinson Sánchez slid the ball into his own net from Ryan Bertrand's teasing cross.

Saints then secured their place in the last 16 of the cup, exacting revenge on Watford thanks to Jack Stephens's first goal for the club.

Stephens was on target again four days later, but this time a home draw was not deemed satisfactory as Saints missed the chance to leapfrog Brighton.

JANUARY

>> FIXTURES <<

SAINTS 1-2 CRYSTAL PALACE Ⓛ

FULHAM 0-1 SAINTS Ⓦ
FA CUP R3

WATFORD 2-2 SAINTS Ⓓ

SAINTS 1-1 TOTTENHAM Ⓓ

SAINTS 1-0 WATFORD Ⓦ
FA CUP R4

SAINTS 1-1 BRIGHTON Ⓓ

>> LEAGUE <<

16	Stoke	25	-25	24
17	Huddersfield	25	-25	24
18	SAINTS	25	-11	23
19	Swansea	25	-18	23
20	West Brom	25	-15	20

MOMENT OF THE MONTH

Jack Stephens marks his 24th birthday with his first goal for the club against Watford.

T he first of two trips to The Hawthorns in the space of a fortnight saw West Brom pay tribute to legendary forward Cyrille Regis, but Saints were in no mood to follow the script and ran out 3-2 winners.

Jack Stephens was among the scorers for a third game running, finding the net either side of Mario Lemina's piledriver and a low free-kick from the similarly in-form James Ward-Prowse.

The visit of Liverpool to St Mary's presented a very different challenge, and Jürgen Klopp's men had the game won by half-time with Roberto Firmino and Mo Salah on target.

Back at West Brom in the cup, Saints found themselves in the quarter-finals thanks to goals from Wesley Hoedt and Dušan Tadić – the latter set up by January signing Guido Carrillo.

Saints signed off the month with a vital late equaliser at Burnley, scored by substitute Manolo Gabbiadini, to hoist themselves out of the bottom three.

FEBRUARY

>> FIXTURES <<

WEST BROM 2-3 **SAINTS** Ⓦ

SAINTS 0-2 **LIVERPOOL** Ⓛ

WEST BROM 1-2 **SAINTS** Ⓦ
FA CUP R5

BURNLEY 1-1 **SAINTS** Ⓓ

>> LEAGUE <<

14	Huddersfield	28	-23	30
15	Newcastle	28	-11	29
16	SAINTS	28	-12	27
17	Crystal Palace	28	-18	27
18	Swansea	28	-20	27

MOMENT OF THE MONTH

James Ward-Prowse's free-kick at West Brom extends Saints' unbeaten run to six games.

A month to spark renewed optimism but ultimately more frustration saw Mauricio Pellegrino replaced as manager by Mark Hughes.

Saints did everything but score in Pellegrino's final home match in charge, as Jack Butland proved unbeatable in the Stoke goal and the Potters held out for a goalless draw, before a 3-0 defeat at Newcastle signalled the end of his reign.

Hughes arrived with Saints just 90 minutes from Wembley, as League One high-fliers Wigan – who sent Man City packing to reach the quarter-finals – eyed another Premier League scalp.

It was a day of firsts for Saints, as the new boss marked his first game at the helm with a first win thanks to first goals for the club from Pierre-Emile Højbjerg and Cédric.

Confidence restored, Saints were unable to build on their cup success in the league, as West Ham scored three times in the first half to ease the unrest at the London Stadium.

MARCH

> FIXTURES <

SAINTS 0-0 **STOKE** (D)

NEWCASTLE 3-0 **SAINTS** (L)

WIGAN 0-2 **SAINTS** (W)
FA CUP QF

WEST HAM 3-0 **SAINTS** (L)

>> LEAGUE <<

16	Huddersfield	32	-28	31
17	Crystal Palace	32	-19	30
18	SAINTS	31	-18	28
19	Stoke	32	-32	27
20	West Brom	32	-26	20

MOMENT OF THE MONTH

Pierre-Emile Højbjerg's first Saints goal helps the club seal a return to Wembley.

With time running out for Saints to save themselves from the drop, the fixture list was hardly aiding their cause.

Games against Arsenal and Chelsea produced heartening displays but ultimately the same result, as a more adventurous Saints were beaten 3-2 on both occasions – even after Jan Bednarek marked his Premier League debut with a goal to put them 2-0 up against the Blues.

Saints had to pick themselves up for the trip to Leicester, where a more conservative approach earned a first point under Mark Hughes, before Chelsea provided the opposition again for the club's first FA Cup semi-final since 2003.

Controversially denied what appeared a legitimate equaliser at Wembley, Saints were beaten 2-0 by the cup winners in waiting.

Now focused solely on staying up, Hughes's men gave their survival hopes a huge boost with victory over Bournemouth, as Dušan Tadić struck either side of half time to secure a first win in nine Premier League outings.

APRIL

> FIXTURES <

ARSENAL 3-2 **SAINTS** Ⓛ

SAINTS 2-3 **CHELSEA** Ⓛ

LEICESTER 0-0 **SAINTS** Ⓓ

CHELSEA 2-0 **SAINTS** Ⓛ
FA CUP SF

SAINTS 2-1 **BOURNEMOUTH** Ⓦ

>> LEAGUE <<

16	Huddersfield	35	-29	35
17	Swansea	35	-25	33
18	SAINTS	35	-19	32
19	Stoke	35	-33	30
20	West Brom	35	-24	28

MOMENT OF THE MONTH

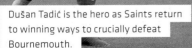

Dušan Tadić is the hero as Saints return to winning ways to crucially defeat Bournemouth.

With three games to go and survival in their own hands, Saints knew they must beat Swansea in the second of those to prevent a decisive final day meeting with Man City.

First up was a trip to Everton, where a draw felt like a defeat after victory was snatched away with virtually the last kick of the game.

A controversial hotel booking cancellation made the headlines as Saints' Swansea preparations were disrupted, merely adding fuel to the fire on a tense night in south Wales.

With a draw more helpful to the hosts, a cagey game ensued, but Saints kept their clean sheet intact before Manolo Gabbiadini pounced soon after his arrival off the bench to send the travelling fans into ecstasy.

Needing a ten-goal swing to save themselves, Swansea could produce no such miracle, and Saints were unlucky to lose even by the narrowest of margins as Gabriel Jesus struck late to take the visitors to 100 Premier League points.

MAY

>> FIXTURES <<

EVERTON 1-1 SAINTS Ⓓ

SWANSEA 0-1 SAINTS Ⓦ

SAINTS 0-1 MAN CITY Ⓛ

>> LEAGUE <<

16	Huddersfield	38	-30	37
17	SAINTS	38	-19	36
18	Swansea	38	-28	33
19	Stoke	38	-33	33
20	West Brom	38	-25	31

MOMENT OF THE MONTH

More like moment of the season, as Manolo Gabbiadini strikes to virtually secure safety.

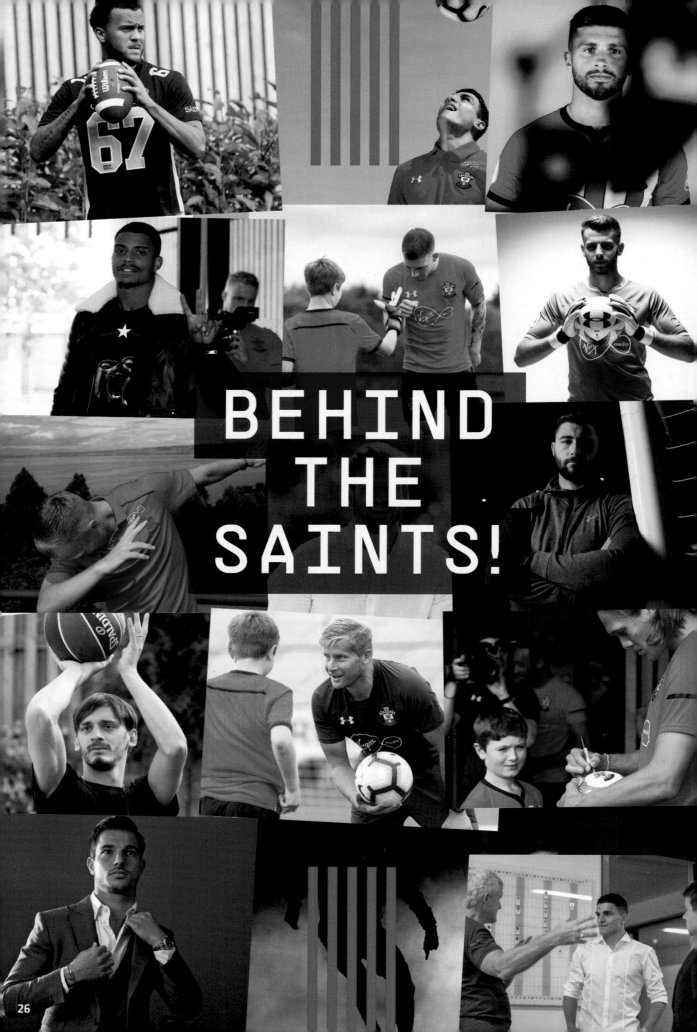

BEHIND THE SAINTS!

PLAYER AWARDS

PLAYER OF THE SEASON

Goalkeeper **Alex McCarthy** was the big winner as the club's end-of-season awards were handed out after the final match of the campaign against Manchester City.

McCarthy was voted as Under Armour Fans' Player of the Season, winning the supporters' poll by a resounding margin, and also recognised by his teammates with the Players' Player of the Season prize.

GOAL OF THE SEASON

The Sure Goal of the Season award went to what was undoubtedly the most meaningful strike of the whole campaign, as **Manolo Gabbiadini**'s effort at Swansea came top of the fans' poll.

Gabbiadini's close-range finish, whilst not the most spectacular, all but secured Saints' Premier League status and will live long in the memory of supporters.

PRESIDENT'S CHOICE AWARD

Each season, honorary club president and Saints' record appearance holder, Terry Paine, selects his player of the season.

Paine often chooses to highlight one of the more unsung members of the team, and this year honoured improving defender **Jack Stephens** for his performances and commitment to the club.

YOUNG PLAYER OF THE SEASON

A winner for the second year running, **Jake Vokins** continued to prove himself as a potential first-team left-back in years to come by earning the Young Player of the Season award.

Still only 18, the England youth international impressed with his performances for the club's Under-18 and Under-23 sides throughout the campaign.

GIRLS' REGIONAL TALENT CLUB PLAYER OF THE SEASON

Kiera Skeels was recognised for her performances in the women's game by succeeding Phoebe Williams as the Girls' Regional Talent Club Player of the Season.

Saints' Regional Talent Club was set up in 2016, and has gone from strength to strength in that time, with a number of players earning international call-ups.

KATHARINA LIEBHERR AWARD

Pierre-Emile Højbjerg was honoured with a new award given on behalf of Katharina Liebherr for a player who has made notable strides in their game and had a major impact on the season.

The Dane has become a popular figure among teammates and supporters alike, for his wholehearted approach and commitment to the cause.

1 How many first-team players did Saints sign in the 2017 summer transfer window?

2 Who were the only team to beat Saints in pre-season?

3 Who scored Saints' first and last goal of 2017/18?

4 Who knocked Saints out of the Carabao Cup, inflicting the club's only August defeat?

5 Name the venue for Saints' first away win of the campaign.

6 Who scored twice in the 2-2 draw with Newcastle in October?

7 Who celebrated their first Premier League start of the season with a brace?

8 In which month did Saints occupy a top-half position in the table for the last time?

9 Charlie Austin started five consecutive league games in the lead up to Christmas, finding the net in four of those. Which team didn't he score against?

10 Who were Saints' opponents on Boxing Day?

11 Alex McCarthy made his Premier League debut for Saints against which club?

12 Who scored Saints' first goal of 2018?

13 Who scored twice in Saints' first away game of the new year?

14 Who was the club's only January signing?

15 How many games did Saints draw in the Premier League; 10, 12 or 15?

16 Who ended his long wait for a Saints goal by scoring in three consecutive games?

17 Which two players scored in Mark Hughes's first match in charge?

18 How many FA Cup ties did Saints win?

19 Who marked their Premier League debut with a goal at St Mary's?

20 Nathan Redmond scored his only goal of the season against which club?

Answers on page 62

29

1   SOFIANE BOUFAL *vs West Brom (H)*

Saints were being held by West Brom with time running out when Boufal embarked on a long run from midway inside his own half. Jinking past four defenders en route to the edge of the box, the enigmatic Moroccan dispatched a cool, side-footed finish into the bottom corner to lay claim to one of the greatest goals ever scored at St Mary's.

DUŠAN TADIĆ *vs Bournemouth (H)*   2

A goal of equal skill and significance that helped Saints secure a first home league win in five months, taking a major step towards survival in the process. Picking up possession just inside the Bournemouth half, Tadić skipped beyond one defender and strode towards goal, letting fly with an improvised toe poke from 18 yards to beat Asmir Begović down to his right.

3   MARIO LEMINA *vs West Brom (A)*

Saints got the better of West Brom three times in 2017/18, scoring a couple of memorable goals along the way. In the league meeting at The Hawthorns, Lemina picked his moment to open his Saints account with the equaliser shortly before half-time. Teed up by Sofiane Boufal, the midfielder took a touch and sent an explosive drive whistling into the top corner from 30 yards.

MANOLO GABBIADINI *vs Swansea (A)*   4

Quite simply the most important goal of Saints' season. Needing victory at Swansea to virtually guarantee Premier League survival, Gabbiadini was summoned from the bench to replace the stricken Jan Bednarek. Four minutes later, the Italian was in the right place at the right time to force the ball home after Łukas Fabiański parried Charlie Austin's snapshot.

5   MAYA YOSHIDA *vs Stoke (A)*

With Saints trailing at Stoke, Yoshida was the man to provide some inspiration with a stunning volley to draw the team level. Receiving the ball on the left, Sofiane Boufal beat his man and crossed to Shane Long, who helped it on for Yoshida to acrobatically connect with a scissor kick from eight yards to beat Jack Butland via the underside of the crossbar.

1 RYAN BERTRAND *vs Chelsea (H)*

Saints produced some fine moves to unlock the Premier League's best defences – none more so than this one. From a position deep inside his own half, Bertrand played a short pass and took off down the left. When Wesley Hoedt found Pierre-Emile Højbjerg, the Dane spotted the run of Bertrand, who galloped into the Chelsea box to set up Dušan Tadić for a simple tap-in.

JAMES WARD-PROWSE *vs Chelsea (H)* **2**

Already in pole position thanks to Dušan Tadić's opener, there seemed minimal danger when Saints were awarded a free-kick 40 yards from goal. Only one man could manufacture a set-piece opportunity from such a position, and up stepped Ward-Prowse to send a perfect delivery to the far post for Jan Bednarek to score on his Premier League debut.

3 SOFIANE BOUFAL *vs Man City (A)*

Saints had given a very decent account of themselves at the Etihad Stadium, but still trailed with 15 minutes to go. Enter substitute Boufal, the architect behind the equaliser. Ryan Bertrand more than did his bit, digging out a cross from near the corner flag that was met by Boufal with a cushioned first touch that bought him a yard of space to pick out Oriol Romeu.

DUŠAN TADIĆ *vs Arsenal (H)* **4**

The Gunners were on the receiving end twice in the season, as Saints started like a train at St Mary's. Charlie Austin fed the ball into Tadić, who cleverly rolled his man to open up space ahead of him. The only player in support was Austin behind him, so Tadić waited for the striker to run beyond him before playing a delightful reverse pass into his stride.

5 CÉDRIC *vs Arsenal (A)*

The trip to Arsenal in early April showcased a more adventurous Saints under Mark Hughes. Trailing 2-1, the new boss encouraged his players to push forward and they got their rewards. The equaliser owed much to Cédric, who traded passes with Dušan Tadić and skipped past former Saint Calum Chambers before putting the ball on a plate for Charlie Austin.

TOP FIVE SAVES

1 ALEX MCCARTHY *vs Bournemouth (H)*

A save of critical importance, Saints were closing in on victory against Bournemouth at St Mary's with the visitors pressing hard for a last-gasp leveller. When the ball was laid off for Ryan Fraser to strike, Cédric's attempted block sent the shot looping towards the top corner and seemingly out of reach until McCarthy intervened with a stunning stop.

ALEX MCCARTHY *vs Swansea (A)* **2**

It was crunch time for Saints as they went in at half time goalless. A tense game at the Liberty Stadium always seemed likely to be decided by a single goal, so when Jordan Ayew let fly early in the second period, the travelling Saints fans may have feared the worst. Ayew's 25-yard shot was dipping in, only for the backpedalling McCarthy to tip it over.

3 ALEX MCCARTHY *vs Everton (A)*

With Saints holding a 1-0 lead in stoppage time in their penultimate away game, the stakes were high when Leighton Baines stood over a free-kick in prime shooting range. The Everton left-back could hardly have struck it sweeter, as he sent his kick over the wall and towards the top corner, but McCarthy stretched out a strong right hand to repel the danger.

FRASER FORSTER *vs Arsenal (H)* **4**

Saints had taken an early lead against Arsenal and dominated the opening exchanges, but when the Gunners responded, Forster had to be alert to keep Saints' advantage intact. Alexis Sánchez's low cross was met with a fierce first-time shot from Aaron Ramsey, which sent the keeper sprawling to his left to make a brilliant one-handed save.

5 FRASER FORSTER *vs Stoke (A)*

The only penalty save of Saints' season was made by Forster to deny his future boss Mark Hughes, then in charge of Stoke. Facing Saido Berahino in the 43rd minute, Forster guessed correctly, diving to his left and beating the ball away with both hands. The save extended Berahino's miserable scoreless run in a Stoke shirt to 30 Premier League games.

TOP FIVE MATCHES

1 SWANSEA 0-1 SAINTS

Not the most entertaining, this was a game littered with tension that defined both teams' seasons. The mysterious cancellation of Saints' hotel booking added fuel to the fire, but the match itself would prove a slow burner. Alex McCarthy saved brilliantly from Jordan Ayew early in the second half, before substitute Manolo Gabbiadini pounced to virtually secure survival.

SAINTS 2-1 BOURNEMOUTH 2

The win that set up Saints' great escape came at the expense of south coast neighbours Bournemouth, who threw everything at Mark Hughes's men in a nervy finale. Dušan Tadić was the hero, twice putting Saints in front, including a clever toe-poke to win the game. Alex McCarthy's heroic save from Ryan Fraser's deflected shot in stoppage time was crucial.

3 SAINTS 4-1 EVERTON

Perhaps Saints' best performance of the season saw Everton brushed aside at St Mary's. Dušan Tadić raced through on goal to open the scoring, before Gylfi Sigurdsson struck with a bolt from the blue to equalise. It would take a pair of near-post headers from Charlie Austin to put Saints back in control, before Steven Davis put the icing on the cake.

WEST BROM 2-3 SAINTS 4

Having slipped into the relegation zone and fallen behind at rock bottom West Brom, Saints needed a big response. Mario Lemina's stunning shot from distance was quickly followed by Jack Stephens's third goal in three games, before James Ward-Prowse fired in a low free-kick. Back came Albion, as Salomón Rondón headed home, but Saints held on for three precious points.

5 SAINTS 3-2 WEST HAM

Having drawn a blank on the opening day, Saints were determined to get a first win on the board against West Ham. Two goals to the good in the first half against ten men, Saints were cruising to victory, only for the Hammers to respond with a brace from Javier Hernández. When Saints were awarded a stoppage-time penalty, Charlie Austin rolled it in to save the day.

TEAMMATES

SAINTS PLAYERS LOVE NOTHING MORE THAN TO DISH THE DIRT ON THEIR TEAMMATES. WE ASKED A FEW PROBING QUESTIONS TO SEE WHAT WE COULD FIND OUT ABOUT THE SQUAD...

WHO IS THE JOKER?

RB: There's a circle of bandits and I'm definitely in the circle! The others are probably Redders (Nathan Redmond) and Charlie.

JS: Chaz (Charlie Austin). He's not very funny, but he's always laughing and joking with himself. He's always sending me videos, as well, but some are funnier than others.

QUICKEST PLAYER?

RB: At the moment, funnily enough, Charlie is on top. It must've been downhill!

AM: Over a short distance, Charlie is up there. But overall, I'd say Longy.

JS: Chaz reckons it's him, but it's definitely not, even if the stats apparently say so! It's probably Shane.

WORST DRESS SENSE?

RB: Oriol Romeu. Horrendous. I'm confident if you saw him now, you would see what I mean. Ori has the worst gear, Cédric the tightest gear and Gabbi the loosest gear.

WH: Anyone who comes into training in a tracksuit!

OR: I will pick Cédric. It's so tight I don't know how he breathes!

RYAN BERTRAND

JACK STEPHENS

ALEX MCCARTHY

AM: Oriol. Some of his gear is dreadful. The other day he looked like he was ready to play golf – he was wearing Ian Poulter trousers and riding boots!

NR: Ori comes in with some cargo pants sometimes, which are a bit questionable.

JS: Ori. It's all over the place, but he loves it. At least he's enjoying it.

WHO IS THE MOST INTELLIGENT?

RB: Academically, probably Fraser, but Charlie won some sports quiz the other day. He's a bit of a quizmaster, so if I'm doing pub quizzes, I want Charlie in my team. If I'm talking lectures, I'll pick Fraser!

LEAST INTELLIGENT?

JS: Matt Targett. Sorry mate, but that's an easy one!

BEST DANCER?

WH: I've seen Nathan Redmond dance a lot. He's pretty good, so it's got to be him.

NR: Me. Mario says he's alright, but I'm still not sure. Cuco Martina was a good dancer!

BEST PRANK?

WH: I had a teammate in Holland who made so many jokes in the changing room I could make a book out of it! One of them was to take all your stuff – socks, shoes, clothes, bag – and tie it all together and put it on the ceiling.

NR: There was one at Norwich. Ricky van Wolfswinkel used to bring party poppers in and tie them to the inside of your locker, so when you opened it, they would just pop up in your face! I've not seen one like that here yet.

YOU ARE STRANDED WITH ONE TEAMMATE, WHO DO YOU CHOOSE?

WH: I hope that never happens! If I have to choose, I would pick Manolo Gabbiadini so I can speak Italian with him.

OR: I will pick Maya, because he cooks amazing sushi!

NR: Berty (Ryan Bertrand). He'll help me forget that I'm on an island because he makes me laugh so much. Sometimes he talks a lot of rubbish, but he can be quite smart.

WESLEY HOEDT

ORIOL ROMEU

NATHAN REDMOND

TOP OF THE SAINTS 2017/18

7
GOALS
AUSTIN

4
ASSISTS
BERTRAND

41
APPEARANCES
TADIC

3136
MINUTES
BERTRAND

48
SHOTS
AUSTIN

1843
PASSES
ROMEU

2357
TOUCHES
BERTRAND

159
CROSSES
WARD-PROWSE

93
TACKLES
ROMEU

69
INTERCEPTIONS
ROMEU

172
CLEARANCES
HOEDT

68
SAVES
FORSTER

SAINTS PUZZLES

CAN YOU ANSWER ALL 10 QUESTIONS CORRECTLY TO UNLOCK THE ANSWER?

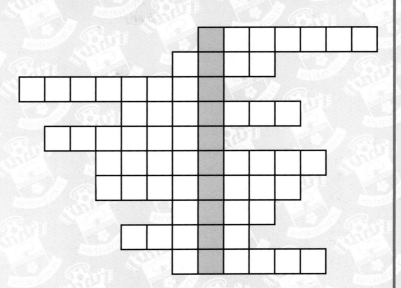

1/ Which former Saint is the Premier League's all-time top goalscorer?

2/ Which Saints Academy graduate scored twice in the 2018 Champions League final?

3/ Which team did Saints beat three times in 2017/18?

4/ Pierre-Emile Højbjerg hails from which country?

5/ Where did Saints play on Boxing Day 2017?

6/ Who is the only player to score more than 100 Premier League goals for Saints?

7/ Which Saint scored a goal at the 2018 World Cup?

8/ What was Mark Hughes's shirt number when he played for Saints?

9/ Saints faced German side Schalke in which country?

10/ Who scored Saints' most famous goal – the winner in the 1976 FA Cup final?

FIND THE WORDS IN THE GRID

Words can go horizontally, vertically and diagonally in all eight directions.

ACADEMY
ASSIST
GOAL
HUGHES
PENALTY
PREMIER LEAGUE
RED CARD
STAPLEWOOD
ST MARY'S
THE DELL
UNDER ARMOUR
WE MARCH ON

E	U	G	A	E	L	R	E	I	M	E	R	P
R	U	O	M	R	A	R	E	D	N	U	Y	F
S	T	A	P	L	E	W	O	O	D	T	X	W
N	D	C	N	T	R	H	Z	L	L	F	E	V
B	R	A	L	S	D	P	U	A	K	M	J	D
L	A	D	L	I	Q	G	N	G	A	T	G	R
M	C	E	E	S	G	E	J	R	H	N	N	S
H	D	M	D	S	P	N	C	W	G	E	Y	Y
H	E	Y	E	A	D	H	F	L	K	R	S	L
L	R	Z	H	F	O	B	L	C	A	F	V	L
R	M	V	T	N	N	M	L	M	R	O	N	Q
M	R	D	R	M	B	M	T	M	T	N	G	Z
M	R	Y	H	M	M	S	R	D	N	M	X	B

Answers on page 62.

STUART ARMSTRONG

STATS

BORN: 30 MARCH 1992
POSITION: ATTACKING MIDFIELDER
CONTRACT: 2022
FORMER CLUB: CELTIC
APPEARANCES: 142
GOALS: 27
NATIONAL TEAM: SCOTLAND
CAPS: 6
GOALS: 1

Correct as of end of 2017/18 season.

HE SAID

"Watching from afar, I've enjoyed the attractive football Southampton play. It's an attacking style and that's a big part of my game. Every season, I put demands on myself and set targets to create and score."

WE SAID

"It is important we add a greater goal threat to the team as a whole, and to our midfield specifically, and Stuart's record of scoring and creating makes him an extremely exciting addition in that area." – Mark Hughes

DID YOU KNOW?

Armstrong was given his Scotland debut by ex-Saints boss Gordon Strachan in a World Cup qualifier against Slovenia in March 2017. Strachan later declared his performance "the best Scotland debut I've ever seen".

ANGUS GUNN

STATS

BORN: 22 JANUARY 1996
POSITION: GOALKEEPER
CONTRACT: 2023
FORMER CLUB: NORWICH (ON LOAN FROM MAN CITY)
APPEARANCES: 51
GOALS: 0
NATIONAL TEAM: ENGLAND U21S
CAPS: 11
GOALS: 0

Correct as of end of 2017/18 season.

HE SAID

"I want to push for the No. 1 spot straightaway. I've come to play Premier League football and I'll be doing everything in my power in training to get that. For me, the ultimate dream would be to play for England."

WE SAID

"There was a lot of interest from other teams in the Premier League, so for Angus to choose Southampton as the best option for him is another positive indication of the work the club is doing and what is being built here." – Mark Hughes

DID YOU KNOW?

Gunn was called up to England's pre-World Cup training camp by Gareth Southgate, who sees the youngster as a potential No. 1 in the future. Southgate was Gunn's manager at Under-21 level.

MOHAMED ELYOUNOUSSI

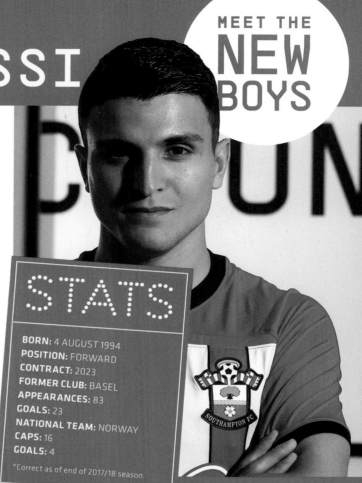

HE SAID

"I'm a hard worker on the pitch and I like to create chances, either for me or to play others through. That's where I'm at my best, when I can use my creativity, so I think the philosophy of the club will suit me very well."

WE SAID

"Mohamed is a very exciting addition to our attacking options. He has got an outstanding record of goals and assists in two different countries, and we have been extremely impressed by the intelligence he has shown in his play." – Mark Hughes

DID YOU KNOW?

Mohamed, nickname "Moi", was born in Morocco and is the cousin of fellow Norway international Tarik Elyounoussi. Tarik, six years older, is an attacking midfielder who plays for AIK in Sweden.

STATS

BORN: 4 AUGUST 1994
POSITION: FORWARD
CONTRACT: 2023
FORMER CLUB: BASEL
APPEARANCES: 83
GOALS: 23
NATIONAL TEAM: NORWAY
CAPS: 16
GOALS: 4

*Correct as of end of 2017/18 season.

JANNIK VESTERGAARD

HE SAID

"Every Danish guy loves to see himself in the Premier League – it is the biggest league in the world and a very attractive place to play as a Danish footballer. It has always been a dream – it is a dream – and I'm looking forward to it."

WE SAID

"One of our intentions this summer was to strengthen our aerial presence, and Jannik can help us do that not only defensively, but also in the opposition penalty area. His character and leadership qualities have been impressive." – Mark Hughes

DID YOU KNOW?

At two metres tall (6ft 7in), Vestergaard has become the tallest player in the Premier League. The Dane was also the tallest outfield player at the World Cup, second only to Croatian goalkeeper Lovre Kalinić.

STATS

BORN: 3 AUGUST 1992
POSITION: CENTRAL DEFENDER
CONTRACT: 2022
FORMER CLUB: BORUSSIA MÖNCHENGLADBACH
APPEARANCES: 83
GOALS: 7
NATIONAL TEAM: DENMARK
CAPS: 16
GOALS: 1

*Correct as of end of 2017/18 season.

DANNY INGS

Danny Ings became Southampton's fifth and final major signing of the summer, arriving from Liverpool on transfer deadline day on a season-long loan, ahead of a permanent move next summer.

Ings began his career further along the south coast, with Bournemouth, before moving to Burnley in 2011, where he went on to make 130 appearances and scored 43 goals for the Clarets.

A crucial member of Burnley's 2013/14 promotion-winning season, Ings's good form continued in the Premier League, earning a move to Anfield in 2015. Although he was restricted by injury, the forward impressed during his time on the pitch on Merseyside, also earning a first England cap against Lithuania.

HE SAID
"I'm over the moon to come home and be close to my family. When this football club came up, I had to take the opportunity. I felt it was time to start a new journey for me. I want to show what I'm about again."

WE SAID
"We have admired Danny for some time now, not only for his ability, but also his character and personality, which we feel will be an ideal fit in our dressing room. He's a local boy, who gives us another excellent option up front."
– Mark Hughes

DID YOU KNOW?
Born in Winchester, boyhood Saints fan Ings grew up in Netley and was briefly on the club's books as a schoolboy, before turning professional at Bournemouth. He won Championship Player of the Year at Burnley in 2013/14.

STATS

BORN: 23 JULY 1992
POSITION: FORWARD
CONTRACT: 2019 (LOAN)
FORMER CLUB: LIVERPOOL
APPEARANCES: 25
GOALS: 4
NATIONAL TEAM: ENGLAND
CAPS: 1
GOALS: 0

*Correct as of end of 2017/18 season.

MARK HUGHES

Southampton confirmed Mark Hughes had signed a new three-year contract as the club's First Team Manager in the summer, after the Welshman successfully guided Saints to Premier League survival last season.

Hughes inherited a tricky position when initially appointed on a short-term deal in March, when Saints were fighting to avoid relegation with just eight matches to play, including fixtures against Arsenal, Chelsea and Man City.

But crucial victories over Bournemouth and Swansea all but secured safety, and Hughes maintained his proud record of never being relegated as a player or manager. In the nine Premier League seasons that he has led a club from start to finish, eight of those have resulted in a top-half finish.

HE SAID
"Mark (Bowen), Eddie (Niedzwiecki) and I are thrilled to have signed long-term contracts with the club. The staff and the players will work hard every day to deliver the success this club deserves, and with everyone pulling together we will achieve our goals."

WE SAID
"It just feels like the right hire at the right time for the club. The decision to go with Mark in the time frame that we had to meet him and to bring him in was very tight, but everything since they've been here has been natural and the fit has been perfect." – Ralph Krueger

DID YOU KNOW?
Hughes has managed more Premier League games (452*) than any other boss currently in the division. He ranks sixth on the all-time list, behind only Arsène Wenger, Sir Alex Ferguson, Harry Redknapp, David Moyes and Sam Allardyce.

STATS

BORN: 1 NOVEMBER 1963
PLAYING POSITION: CENTRE FORWARD
FORMER CLUBS: 1980-86 MANCHESTER UNITED
1986-88 BARCELONA
1987-88 BAYERN MUNICH (LOAN)
1988-95 MANCHESTER UNITED
1995-98 CHELSEA
1998-00 SOUTHAMPTON
2000 EVERTON
2000-02 BLACKBURN ROVERS

APPEARANCES: 799
GOALS: 224
NATIONAL TEAM: WALES
CAPS: 72
GOALS: 224
TEAMS MANAGED:
1999-04 WALES
2004-08 BLACKBURN ROVERS
2008-09 MANCHESTER CITY
2010-11 FULHAM
2012 QPR
2013-18 STOKE CITY
2018- SOUTHAMPTON
GAMES MANAGED: 593*
WINS: 226* (38%)

*Correct as of end of 2017/18 season.

KIT LAUNCH DAY!

SOUTHAMPTON'S EYE-CATCHING UNDER ARMOUR HOME AND AWAY KITS FOR THE 2018/19 SEASON WERE DEBUTED IN A SPECIAL GAME BETWEEN TWO LOCAL JUNIOR SIDES – ROMSEY TOWN YOUTH FC AND LITTLETON JUNIORS FC.

The unsuspecting youngsters were surprised with the new kits after walking into their dressing rooms, which had been given a complete transformation by the club and Under Armour.

On top of that, they also received a shock visit from Saints legends Matt Le Tissier and Franny Benali, who managed the teams for the day.

Both strips once again feature the latest, cutting-edge Under Armour technology, with this year's stylish home shirt featuring traditional red and white stripes, with an all-red back, sleeves and shoulders, as well as black shorts and red and black socks.

The away kit takes inspiration from the past, with the club producing a brand new yellow and blue strip, reminiscent of what was worn in Saints' famous 1976 FA Cup victory.

Also released is the new blue goalkeeper kit, along with a striking third kit – a clever twist on the classic-style home version, integrating a darker tone of red that retains the feel of the club's traditional stripes, while it is offset by a smart, black trim.

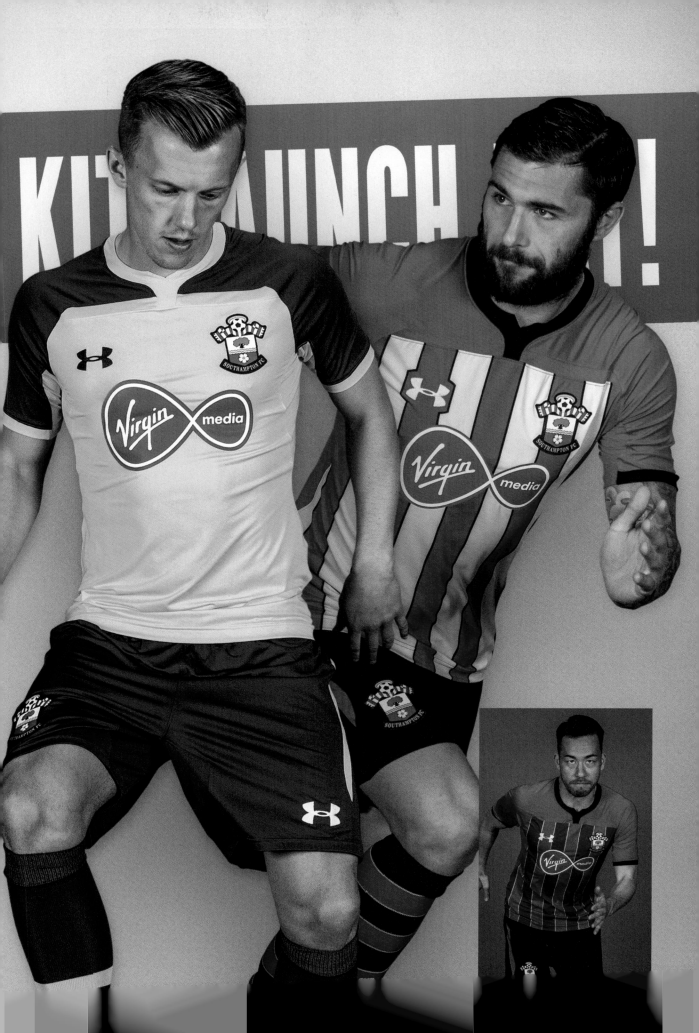

PRE-SEASON WITH SAINTS!

NAME THE OPPOSITION!

CAN YOU NAME WHICH TEAM THESE SAINTS STARS HAVE JUST SCORED AGAINST?

1 PIERRE-EMILE HØJBJERG

2 JAN BEDNAREK

3 MANOLO GABBIADINI

4 CHARLIE AUSTIN

5 JAMES WARD-PROWSE

6 SHANE LONG

Answers on page 62.

STEVEN DAVIS

JAMES WARD-PROWSE

FOOTBALL
Memories

WE ASKED A COLLECTION OF SAINTS PLAYERS TO CAST THEIR MINDS BACK TO THEIR CHILDHOOD DAYS STARTING OUT IN FOOTBALL, TO FIND OUT HOW THEY BECAME THE PLAYERS WE SEE TODAY...

WHAT IS YOUR EARLIEST FOOTBALL MEMORY?

PEH: Playing in the park with my dad or my friends, standing really far apart and just kicking the ball as hard as I could!

JWP: I remember going to watch a local team in the National League South. I managed to get the ball on the side of the pitch and throw it back to one of the players to take a throw-in. That was quite a special moment – just to touch the football as a spectator.

SD: I just remember kicking a ball about with my brother, who's three years older than me – I was always out playing with him.

C: I remember my first training session in the stadium of Sporting, when I was seven years old. I went inside the dressing room and all the players were there. I was very nervous!

DO YOU REMEMBER YOUR FIRST FOOTBALL KIT OR PAIR OF BOOTS?

PEH: I think it was a Zinedine Zidane shirt, made in somewhere I can't say! It was so fake but I never took it off. It was a Real Madrid shirt with the number five on the back.

JWP: I think I had an England kit with Beckham on the back. My first pair of boots were the Predator Champagne boots – they were always the standout pair from my childhood.

SD: My first kit was a Rangers kit, being a fan of them, and my first pair of boots were the Puma Kings with the big tongue!

C: My first boots were the black Adidas Copa Mundial with green stripes instead of white – I remember those!

WHEN YOU WERE GROWING UP, WHAT POSITION DID YOU PLAY?

PEH: I was a defender but then suddenly became a striker because I was a big boy – quite fat with a big head! I could strike the ball really well.

JWP: I played as a centre-back from when I was 12 until I was 14. I played there for Saints in the Dallas Cup (a youth tournament held in Texas).

SD: We've got a lad playing for Northern Ireland who was a goalkeeper until he was 16, and now he's a striker! My past has been pretty boring compared to that – I was always a midfielder.

C: I played all of my career until I was 16 as an attacking midfielder. After that I started to play at right-back sometimes, but even in the first team at Sporting I started off playing in midfield.

WHAT ADVICE WOULD YOU GIVE YOUR YOUNGER SELF?

PEH: Make mistakes, learn from them, be honest and get better.

JWP: I think just to be prepared for the ups and downs – there are always good times and bad times. I didn't used to deal with the bad times so well.

SD: Work hard and listen to your coaches. My approach has always been to take as much as I can out of every day and to improve every day to make the most of my career.

C: When my friends were going out or staying somewhere late I couldn't join them, and I had a lot of help from my parents on that. For me, this was crucial in everything.

PIERRE-EMILE HØJBJERG

CÉDRIC

THE SAINTS STORE

Available to buy in our Stadium Store, our newly refurbished Westquay Store and online, we've got a great selection of products for every Saints fan. See our top picks below...

**SAINTS
HOME FOOTBALL**
£8

**SAINTS
STEGO DINOSAUR TOY**
£8

**KIDS SEKONDA
WATCH BLACK**
£30

**SAMMY SAINT
NOTEBOOK**
£8

**YOUTH
HOME SHIRT**
£40

**SAINTS LARGE
STATIONERY SET**
£12

**YOUTH
AWAY SHIRT**
£40

**SAINTS SHIRT
LUNCH BAG**
£10

**SAMSON VINTAGE
SCARF BEAR**
£15

**SAMMY SAINT
YOUTH SCARF**
£10

 STORE.SAINTSFC.CO.UK   STADIUM AND WESTQUAY STORES   OFFICIAL DISCOUNTS APPLY*

CHRISTMAS WITH SAINTS!

49

PLAYER PROFILES

ALEX MCCARTHY

1

Age: 28
Position: Goalkeeper
Signed From: Crystal Palace
Joined Saints: 2016
Height: 193cm
Weight: 79kg
Nationality: English
2017/18: Saints' Player of the Year, despite only making his first start in December, keeping a clean sheet at Man Utd.

CÉDRIC

2

Age: 26
Position: Defender
Signed From: Sporting CP
Joined Saints: 2015
Height: 172cm
Weight: 67kg
Nationality: Portuguese
2017/18: Scored his first Saints goal in Hughes's first game in charge – the FA Cup quarter-final at Wigan.

MAYA YOSHIDA

3

Age: 29
Position: Defender
Signed From: VVV-Venlo
Joined Saints: 2012
Height: 189cm
Weight: 78kg
Nationality: Japanese
2017/18: Scored a spectacular scissor-kick against Stoke at the expense of future boss Hughes in September.

JACK STEPHENS

5

Age: 24
Position: Defender
Signed From: Plymouth
Joined Saints: 2011
Height: 185cm
Weight: 75kg
Nationality: English
2017/18: Finally struck his first Saints goal seven years after joining the club, then scored three in three games.

WESLEY HOEDT

6

Age: 24
Position:
Defender
Signed From:
Lazio
Joined Saints: 2017
Height: 188cm
Weight: 77kg
Nationality: Dutch
2017/18:
Started 28 Premier League games in his debut season in England and made his presence felt.

SHANE LONG

7

Age: 31
Position:
Forward
Signed From:
Hull
Joined Saints: 2014
Height: 178cm
Weight: 70kg
Nationality: Irish
2017/18:
Scored Saints' first goal of 2018 – his first of the season – with a sharp finish against Crystal Palace.

STEVEN DAVIS

8

Age: 33
Position:
Midfielder
Signed From: Rangers
Joined Saints: 2012
Height: 173cm
Weight: 70kg
Nationality:
Northern Irish
2017/18:
Scored all four of his goals for club and country before the end of November. Season curtailed by injury.

CHARLIE AUSTIN

10

Age: 29
Position:
Forward
Signed From:
QPR
Joined Saints: 2016
Height: 188cm
Weight: 84kg
Nationality: English
2017/18:
Hit red-hot form with five goals in five starts before injury struck and left him sidelined for three months.

SAM McQUEEN

12

Age: 23
Position:
Defender
Signed From:
Academy
Joined Saints: 2003
Height: 181cm
Weight: 70kg
Nationality: English
2017/18:
Celebrated his only league start of the season with a confident display and clean sheet at Man Utd.

ORIOL ROMEU

14

Age: 26
Position:
Midfielder
Signed From:
Chelsea
Joined Saints: 2015
Height: 183cm
Weight: 83kg
Nationality: Spanish
2017/18:
Typically whole-hearted in midfield, his 11 yellow cards was the highest of any player in the Premier League.

SAM GALLAGHER

15

Age: 22
Position:
Forward
Signed From:
Plymouth
Joined Saints: 2012
Height: 194cm
Weight: 75kg
Nationality: English
2017/18:
Helped Birmingham avoid relegation in a season-long loan spell, including a run of six goals in eight games.

JAMES WARD-PROWSE

16

Age: 23
Position:
Midfielder
Signed From:
Academy
Joined Saints: 2003
Height: 173cm
Weight: 66kg
Nationality: English
2017/18:
Scored four goals in five games in a purple patch at the turn of year, including a trademark free-kick.

MARIO LEMINA

18

Age: 24
Position: Midfielder
Signed From: Juventus
Joined Saints: 2017
Height: 184cm
Weight: 85kg
Nationality: Gabonese
2017/18: Scored with an explosive shot from distance in a crucial 3-2 win at struggling West Brom in February.

HARRISON REED

19

Age: 23
Position: Midfielder
Signed From: Academy
Joined Saints: 2003
Height: 176cm
Weight: 72kg
Nationality: English
2017/18: Made 43 appearances on loan at Norwich, before urging teammate Gunn to rejoin him at St Mary's.

MANOLO GABBIADINI

20

Age: 26
Position: Forward
Signed From: Napoli
Joined Saints: 2017
Height: 181cm
Weight: 72kg
Nationality: Italian
2017/18: Not prolific but scored at crucial times throughout the season, not least the all-important Swansea winner.

RYAN BERTRAND

21

Age: 29
Position: Defender
Signed From: Chelsea
Joined Saints: 2014
Height: 179cm
Weight: 85kg
Nationality: English
2017/18: Captained the team in the absence of Davis and led by example with typical consistency up and down the left flank.

NATHAN REDMOND

22

Age: 24
Position: Midfielder
Signed From: Norwich
Joined Saints: 2016
Height: 173cm
Weight: 69kg
Nationality: English
2017/18: Found his form at just the right time under Hughes, scoring his first goal in nearly a year at Everton.

PIERRE-EMILE HØJBJERG

23

Age: 23
Position: Midfielder
Signed From: Bayern Munich
Joined Saints: 2016
Height: 185cm
Weight: 85kg
Nationality: Danish
2017/18: Joined Cédric in opening his account at Wigan, helping Saints to a first FA Cup semi-final since 2003.

ALFIE JONES

32

Age: 20
Position: Defender
Signed From: Academy
Joined Saints: 2007
Height: 187cm
Weight: 77kg
Nationality: English
2017/18: Celebrated a string of impressive performances for the club's Under-23 side with a new two-year deal.

MATT TARGETT

33

Age: 22
Position: Defender
Signed From: Academy
Joined Saints: 2003
Height: 183cm
Weight: 70kg
Nationality: English
2017/18: Proved Fulham's lucky charm, winning 15 of 21 games while on loan and helping them to promotion.

JAN BEDNAREK

35

Age: 22
Position:
Defender
Signed From:
Lech Poznań
Joined Saints: 2017
Height: 189cm
Weight: 77kg
Nationality: Polish
2017/18:
Scored on his Premier League debut against Chelsea in April and finished the season strongly.

JOSH SIMS

39

Age: 21
Position:
Midfielder
Signed From:
Academy
Joined Saints: 2011
Height: 168cm
Weight: 67kg
Nationality: English
2017/18:
Played his way back into the squad after nine months out with some energetic substitute appearances.

HARRY LEWIS

41

Age: 20
Position:
Goalkeeper
Signed From:
Shrewsbury
Joined Saints: 2015
Height: 191cm
Weight: 77kg
Nationality: English
2017/18:
Kept ten clean sheets on loan at Dundee United, helping them to the Scottish Championship play-offs.

JAKE HESKETH

42

Age: 22
Position:
Midfielder
Signed From:
Academy
Joined Saints: 2006
Height: 168cm
Weight: 63kg
Nationality: English
2017/18:
Creative spark who scored twice against League One side Northampton in the Checkatrade Trophy.

YAN VALERY

43

Age: 19
Position:
Defender
Signed From:
Stade Rennais
Joined Saints: 2015
Height: 183cm
Weight: 79kg
Nationality: French
2017/18:
Impressive young right-back who scored his first goal for the Under-23s before signing a new deal.

FRASER FORSTER

44

Age: 30
Position:
Goalkeeper
Signed From:
Celtic
Joined Saints: 2014
Height: 201cm
Weight: 93kg
Nationality: English
2017/18:
Started the season as first choice, keeping three clean sheets in Saints' first five league games.

PLAYER PROFILES

Accurate as of the end of the 2017/18 season.

WORLD CUP TRIVIA

THERE WERE FOUR REPRESENTATIVES FROM THE CURRENT SOUTHAMPTON SQUAD AT THE WORLD CUP IN RUSSIA. CAN YOU MATCH UP EACH STATEMENT TO THE CORRECT PLAYER?

CÉDRIC

MAYA YOSHIDA

JAN BEDNAREK

JANNIK VESTERGAARD

ANSWERS

1. I PLAYED EVERY MINUTE OF MY COUNTRY'S WORLD CUP CAMPAIGN
2. I WAS NAMED IN THE SQUAD BUT DIDN'T PLAY
3. I PLAYED IN THE GAME THAT SAW THE FIRST HAT-TRICK OF THE TOURNAMENT
4. I SCORED MY FIRST INTERNATIONAL GOAL AT THE WORLD CUP
5. MY COUNTRY WON OUR FIRST GAME AFTER ALREADY BEING ELIMINATED
6. MY COUNTRY SCORED THE FASTEST GOAL OF THE TOURNAMENT
7. I WAS 2-0 UP AGAINST BELGIUM IN THE LAST 16
8. MY COUNTRY WAS TOP OF OUR GROUP UNTIL THE LAST SECONDS OF OUR LAST GAME
9. I WAS CRUELLY KNOCKED OUT ON PENALTIES
10. MY COUNTRY WAS KNOCKED OUT IN THE ONLY GAME I DIDN'T PLAY
11. I EXITED THE COMPETITION AT THE GROUP STAGE
12. I WENT THROUGH TO THE KNOCKOUT STAGE BASED ON FAIR PLAY RANKING
13. AN OPPOSING PLAYER WAS SENT OFF AFTER THREE MINUTES OF MY FIRST MATCH
14. I PLAYED THE FULL 90 MINUTES IN THE COMPETITION'S ONLY 3-3 DRAW
15. I CAME ON AS SUB IN MY COUNTRY'S FIRST MATCH
16. MY COUNTRY WAS INVOLVED IN THE ONLY GOALLESS DRAW
17. MY COUNTRY ARE STILL THE REIGNING EUROPEAN CHAMPIONS
18. CHRISTIAN ERIKSEN OF TOTTENHAM IS MY STAR TEAMMATE
19. I PLAYED AGAINST SOUTH AMERICAN, EUROPEAN AND ASIAN TEAMS
20. I WON MY 88TH CAP IN THE GAME THAT SAW MY COUNTRY ELIMINATED

EAT LIKE A SAINT

ENJOY THESE TWO RECIPES MADE BY OUR FIRST-TEAM CHEF TO MAKE SOME YUMMY ENERGY BARS TO HELP FUEL YOUR TRAINING SESSIONS!

Make sure you check with an adult before making these, and please check ingredients carefully if you have any food allergies or special dietary requirements.

BANANA OAT BARS

WHAT YOU WILL NEED

2 large, very ripe bananas
1 vanilla pod
460g rolled oats
115g pitted, chopped dates
60g honey
1 pinch of salt
20g chopped walnuts
20g chopped hazelnuts
20g chopped pecans

METHOD

• Pre-heat oven to 160°C & lightly grease a 9x9 inch square baking dish with olive oil or butter.

• Mash bananas until smooth.

• Split, scrape and stir in the vanilla.

• Add the oats, dates, salt, nuts and honey.

• Pour into your tray and spread out evenly.

• Bake for approx. 30 minutes or until the edges just begin to crisp.

• Cool and cut into bars, approx. two mouthfuls per bar.

APPLE AND BANANA FLAPJACK BARS

WHAT YOU WILL NEED

30g runny honey
50g butter
2 ripe bananas
1 grated apple
100g raisins
250g oats
70g pumpkin seeds
30g smooth peanut butter

METHOD

• Pre-heat oven to 150°C.

• Add butter, honey & peanut butter to saucepan and heat gently until it becomes runny. Check consistency and add a splash of water if necessary.

• Add grated apple and mash in the bananas.

• Remove from heat and add the rest of the ingredients. Mix well.

• Line baking tray and pour in the mix. Bake for 30-40 minutes.

• Cool and cut into bars, approx. two mouthfuls per bar.

2018/19
JUNIOR
MEMBERSHIP

FROM
£10

WE
MARCH
ON

 PRIORITY
TICKET ACCESS

 WELCOME PACK
& GIFTS

 AND MUCH MORE

VISIT **TICKETS.SAINTSFC.CO.UK** FOR MORE INFORMATION

PROWSEY'S SIX STEPS
TO FREE-KICK SUCCESS

① KNOW YOUR DISTANCE

For me, my perfect distance is about 25 yards out, just left of centre. Not too far, but not too close – just enough room to get the ball up and over the wall, with time to bring it back down and hit the target.

② PLACING THE BALL

Before I place the ball, I like to bounce the ball twice. Then I place the ball with the Nike tick facing up towards the sky. That's just my routine.

③ THE WALK BACK

As I stand over the ball, I take four steps backwards at a 45-degree angle. Then I just shuffle my body a bit to relax myself before I begin my run-up.

④ PICK YOUR SPOT

My last thought before I strike the ball is to identify a section of the goal. I look at the goal, where the shortest and tallest players are in the wall and where the goalkeeper is stood.

⑤ THE STANDING FOOT

As I approach the ball, I plant my left foot just beside it, and then try to generate as much whip and speed as possible on the ball.

⑥ THE STRIKE

As I'm striking the ball, I try to hit the bottom right side of the ball to generate some topspin by brushing up over it. I always liken it to a forehand in tennis, with the way you hit the ball over the net and down inside the baseline – it's the same as going over a wall and down into the goal.

PREMIER LEAGUE FOCUS

AFC BOURNEMOUTH

NICKNAME: The Cherries
GROUND: Vitality Stadium
CAPACITY: 11,360
MANAGER: Eddie Howe
LAST SEASON: 12th
TOP SCORER: Callum Wilson, 9 goals

STAR SIGNING: Jefferson Lerma (Levante)

KEY MAN: 21-year-old midfielder Lewis Cook will hope to build on the form that saw him earn his England debut last season.

ARSENAL

NICKNAME: The Gunners
GROUND: Emirates Stadium
CAPACITY: 59,867
MANAGER: Unai Emery
LAST SEASON: 6th
TOP SCORER: Alexandre Lacazette, 17 goals

STAR SIGNING: Lucas Torreira (Sampdoria)

KEY MAN: Pierre-Emerick Aubameyang only arrived in North London in January, but still managed ten Premier League goals last term.

BRIGHTON & HOVE ALBION

NICKNAME: The Seagulls
GROUND: Amex Stadium
CAPACITY: 30,750
MANAGER: Chris Hughton
LAST SEASON: 15th
TOP SCORER: Glenn Murray, 14 goals

STAR SIGNING: Alireza Jahanbaksh (AZ Alkmaar)

KEY MAN: Brighton are not the most expansive side, so the creativity of Pascal Groß is crucial in finding the goals they need to survive.

BURNLEY

NICKNAME: The Clarets
GROUND: Turf Moor
CAPACITY: 21,800
MANAGER: Sean Dyche
LAST SEASON: 7th
TOP SCORER: Chris Wood, 11 goals

STAR SIGNING: Joe Hart (Man City)

KEY MAN: James Tarkowski brilliantly filled the void vacated by Michael Keane's move to Everton, and remains the defensive linchpin.

CARDIFF CITY

NICKNAME: The Bluebirds
GROUND: Cardiff City Stadium
CAPACITY: 33,280
MANAGER: Neil Warnock
LAST SEASON: Championship, 2nd
TOP SCORER: Junior Hoilett, 11 goals

STAR SIGNING: Bobby Reid (Bristol City)

KEY MAN: Cardiff will rely on a solid base, and powerful defender Sean Morrison is crucial at both ends, chipping in with seven goals last term.

CHELSEA

NICKNAME: The Blues
GROUND: Stamford Bridge
CAPACITY: 41,631
MANAGER: Maurizio Sarri
LAST SEASON: 5th
TOP SCORER: Eden Hazard, 17 goals

STAR SIGNING: Jorginho (Napoli)

KEY MAN: Álvaro Morata needs to score 20-plus goals if Chelsea are to mount a title challenge after failing to shine last season.

CRYSTAL PALACE

NICKNAME: The Eagles
GROUND: Selhurst Park
CAPACITY: 25,456
MANAGER: Roy Hodgson
LAST SEASON: 11th
TOP SCORER: Luka Milivojević, 10 goals

STAR SIGNING: Max Meyer (Schalke)

KEY MAN: Palace's best piece of business was keeping Wilfried Zaha – they failed to win all ten league games he didn't start in 2017/18.

EVERTON

NICKNAME: The Toffees
GROUND: Goodison Park
CAPACITY: 39,572
MANAGER: Marco Silva
LAST SEASON: 8th
TOP SCORER: Wayne Rooney, 11 goals

STAR SIGNING: Richarlison (Watford)

KEY MAN: A summer clear out should pave the way for Gylfi Sigurdsson to make the No. 10 position his own and show his best form.

FULHAM

NICKNAME: The Cottagers
GROUND: Craven Cottage
CAPACITY: 25,700
MANAGER: Slaviša Jokanović
LAST SEASON: Championship, 3rd
TOP SCORER: Ryan Sessegnon, 16 goals

STAR SIGNING: Jean Michael Seri (Nice)

KEY MAN: Skipper Tom Cairney sees more of the ball than anyone, and forms a vital supply line to brilliant youngster Ryan Sessegnon.

HUDDERSFIELD TOWN

NICKNAME: The Terriers
GROUND: John Smith's Stadium
CAPACITY: 24,500
MANAGER: David Wagner
LAST SEASON: 16th
TOP SCORER: Steve Mounié, 9 goals

STAR SIGNING: Adama Diakhaby (Monaco)

KEY MAN: Aaron Mooy is Huddersfield's instrumental playmaker, and his set-piece delivery makes them a threat from every dead ball.

LEICESTER CITY

NICKNAME: The Foxes
GROUND: King Power Stadium
CAPACITY: 32,315
MANAGER: Claude Puel
LAST SEASON: 9th
TOP SCORER: Jamie Vardy, 23 goals

STAR SIGNING: James Maddison (Norwich)

KEY MAN: Leicester fought off the attentions of Manchester United to keep hold of England's star World Cup defender Harry Maguire.

LIVERPOOL

NICKNAME: The Reds
GROUND: Anfield
CAPACITY: 54,074
MANAGER: Jürgen Klopp
LAST SEASON: 4th
TOP SCORER: Mohamed Salah, 44 goals

STAR SIGNING: Naby Keïta (RB Leipzig)

KEY MAN: Liverpool score goals for fun, but will be hoping new Brazilian goalkeeper Alisson helps them keep a few more clean sheets.

MANCHESTER CITY

NICKNAME: The Citizens
GROUND: Etihad Stadium
CAPACITY: 55,097
MANAGER: Pep Guardiola
LAST SEASON: Champions
TOP SCORER: Sergio Agüero, 30 goals

STAR SIGNING: Riyad Mahrez (Leicester)

KEY MAN: Electrifying winger Leroy Sané may feel he has a point to prove after being left out of the Germany World Cup squad.

MANCHESTER UNITED

NICKNAME: The Red Devils
GROUND: Old Trafford
CAPACITY: 74,944
MANAGER: José Mourinho
LAST SEASON: Runners-up
TOP SCORER: Romelu Lukaku, 27 goals

STAR SIGNING: Fred (Shakhtar Donetsk)

KEY MAN: Alexis Sanchez did not look settled after his January move, but should improve after a full pre-season with his new club.

NEWCASTLE UNITED

NICKNAME: The Magpies
GROUND: St James' Park
CAPACITY: 52,354
MANAGER: Rafael Benítez
LAST SEASON: 10th
TOP SCORER: Ayoze Pérez, 10 goals

STAR SIGNING: Kenedy (Chelsea)

KEY MAN: Jamaal Lascelles is developing a reputation as one of the best young defenders in the league and is hunting a first England cap.

TOTTENHAM HOTSPUR

NICKNAME: Spurs
GROUND: Tottenham Hotspur Stadium
CAPACITY: 62,062
MANAGER: Mauricio Pochettino
LAST SEASON: 3rd
TOP SCORER: Harry Kane, 41 goals

STAR SIGNING: N/A

KEY MAN: Christian Eriksen remains the creative linchpin of the Spurs team and the chief provider for prolific England captain Kane.

WATFORD

NICKNAME: The Hornets
GROUND: Vicarage Road
CAPACITY: 21,438
MANAGER: Javi Gracia
LAST SEASON: 14th
TOP SCORER: Abdoulaye Doucouré, 7 goals

STAR SIGNING: Gerard Deulofeu (Barcelona)

KEY MAN: Roberto Pereyra has never quite established himself at Watford, but Javi Gracia has taken a shine to the talented Argentinian.

WEST HAM UNITED

NICKNAME: The Hammers
GROUND: London Stadium
CAPACITY: 57,000
MANAGER: Manuel Pellegrini
LAST SEASON: 13th
TOP SCORER: Marko Arnautović, 11 goals

STAR SIGNING: Felipe Anderson (Lazio)

KEY MAN: Having finally left his Arsenal roots behind, it's a big season for Jack Wilshere, who has the ability to transform West Ham's midfield.

WOLVERHAMPTON WANDERERS

NICKNAME: Wolves
GROUND: Molineux
CAPACITY: 31,700
MANAGER: Nuno Espírito Santo
LAST SEASON: Championship, 1st
TOP SCORER: Diogo Jota, 17 goals

STAR SIGNING: João Moutinho (Monaco)

KEY MAN: Rúben Neves was the talisman of Wolves' promotion year, dictating games with his passing and scoring spectacular goals.

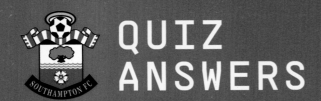

QUIZ ANSWERS

QUIZ OF THE SEASON (P28-29)

1. Three (Jan Bednarek, Mario Lemina, Wesley Hoedt)
2. Augsburg
3. Manolo Gabbiadini
4. Wolves
5. Selhurst Park
6. Manolo Gabbiadini
7. Charlie Austin
8. November
9. Leicester
10. Tottenham
11. Man Utd
12. Shane Long
13. James Ward-Prowse
14. Guido Carrillo
15. 15
16. Jack Stephens
17. Pierre-Emile Højbjerg and Cédric
18. Four
19. Jan Bednarek
20. Everton

WORLD CUP TRIVIA (P54)

1. Maya Yoshida
2. Jannik Vestergaard
3. Cédric
4. Jan Bednarek
5. Jan Bednarek
6. Jannik Vestergaard
7. Maya Yoshida
8. Cédric
9. Jannik Vestergaard
10. Cédric
11. Jan Bednarek
12. Maya Yoshida
13. Maya Yoshida
14. Cédric
15. Jan Bednarek
16. Jannik Vestergaard
17. Cédric
18. Jannik Vestergaard
19. Jan Bednarek
20. Maya Yoshida

HIDDEN WORD (P37)

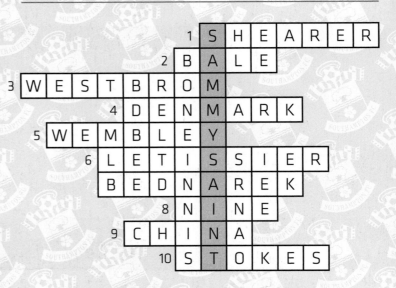

1. SHEARER
2. BALE
3. WESTBROM
4. DENMARK
5. WEMBLEY
6. LETISSIER
7. BEDNAREK
8. NINE
9. CHINA
10. STOKES

Key Answer = **SAMMY SAINT**

WORDSEARCH

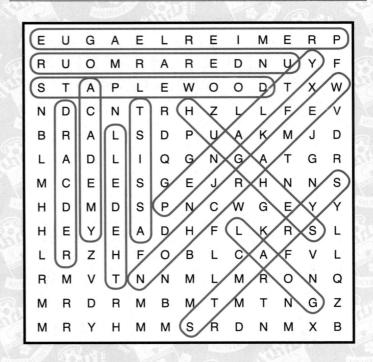

NAME THE OPPOSITION

1. Wigan
2. Chelsea
3. Burnley
4. Bournemouth
5. West Brom
6. Arsenal